Living the Life
of a Prisoner's Wife

Melody M. Jackson

Copyright © 2009 Melody M. Jackson. All rights reserved. No part of this book may be used or reproduced in any manner without written permission from the author except for the use of brief quotation in a book review or scholarly journal.

ISBN: 978-0-692-13566-2

Publisher: Melody M. Jackson

Interior and cover design
by Williams DocuPrep
www.williamsdocuprep.com

Dedication

I dedicate this book to all the families who have loved one in prison.

Contents

Dedication i
Preface 1
Acknowledgements 3
Introduction 5
Chapter I 7
  Caged Bird Set Free 7
    My Secret Rendezvous with Destiny 10
Chapter II 22
  Dawn of A New Beginning 22
    La 'Shonda Elonda 23
    Marriage 31
    Moving Up 35
    The Brownstone Diner 37
    The Cruel and the Cruelty 38
    A New Twist of Fate 44
Chapter III 50
  Revelations 50
    Not the Common but the Uncommon 54

Prison 58

Ministry 67

Chapter IV 70

  A Prisoner's Wife 70

    Ebbing Tides 75

    Jim's Transfer to Atlanta 77

    Year '99 80

    Divorce Action 88

Epilogue 91

  The Gift of Hope 92

  The Gift of Faith 93

  The Gift of Love 94

About the Author 97

Preface

Inspiration is a divine influence, a mental force exerted upon a person that has the capability of stimulating their intellect and emotions to the extent of revealing and communicating highly valued and personal revelations of themselves to others. It comes from various sources: family, relatives, friends, dreams, ideas, a supernatural being or any other inspiring agent akin to life itself. The numerous inspirations heaped upon me were received with a notable amount of skepticism that existed during the passing of many long shadows.

God inspired me to tell my story. I was awakened early one morning from a deep sleep by an unusually authoritative voice that reverberated in my ears like the sound of a distant thunder. God said to me, "I want you to write a book. The book shall be titled: Living the Life of a Prisoner's Wife."

And then the voice was gone as suddenly as it had appeared. My room was filled with an eerie silence. My entire body began to tremble like green leaves on a tree on a breezy summer day.

My family, close relatives and friends served as catalytic agents in boosting me courageously onward to fulfill God's divine directive to me.

I became involved in a teenage romance, unbeknownst to my strict parents. My first child was born out of wedlock. The man who fathered my child displayed all the attributes of a fine gentleman. Subsequently, we were married. Our marriage flourished and blossomed. We were a happy family. Then, for reasons unknown to me my husband began staying away from home for unusually long periods of time. Strange things began to happen. Things beyond my wildest dreams engulfed me in horror and disbelief.

Readers should brace themselves for an encounter with the good, the bad and the ugly; the bitter and sweet; love and hatred. There may be some passages that could be interpreted by some individuals as being morally offensive, objectionable, or even repulsive. Albeit, it is my hope that other wives under similar circumstances, and young ladies in their teens will derive some benefit from my story.

The incidents set forth in this book are true. Some names and places have been changed to protect their identity. The occurrence of certain events has been altered to achieve coherence and the writing of this book.

Acknowledgements

My story would have remained a secret forever locked within my soul were it not for the sacred words spoken to me by our Heavenly Father. His confidence in me and my faith in Him sustain me during the most difficult times of my journey through life, even when I nearly lost all confidence within myself. Therefore, and foremost, I give thanks to Him who instilled the spirit in me to write this book.

Thanks to my husband who persistently urge me to follow my dreams.

A special thanks to my two lovely children La'Shonda and Daymion; I love you very much; also, my granddaughter Genesis Allen the apple of my eye. Their endless love provided me with the much-needed strength and staying power necessary for me to endure the many trials and tribulations thrust upon me for reasons unknown.

Thanks to my daddy and late mother for being good parents and teaching me the way of life, to love and to put God first in my life.

Maurica Scott, my sister-in-law deserves special

attention. She was my nurse and therapist during my illness. She was my inspiring critic from the beginning to the end of my writing this book. Many thanks to all my friends at the American Red Cross for visiting with me during my illness and for supporting me in my endeavor.

I am grateful to all my brothers and sisters, particularly Bibi and Rudy for their untiring and valuable assistance.

My appreciation and gratitude for my great uncle Eugene Sartor is exceeded only by my inability to find suitable words of expression and praise. He stayed on me like ivy on an oak tree to tell my story. Thank you for being my editor in chief. Thank you for sifting through and removing the impurities and textual errors from my story and supplanting them with words of wisdom superior to my own.

Introduction

I am not a storyteller, but I will attempt to relate a succession of incidents that occurred in my life... in my own words. This is not a story that one would sit around an open fire, on a chilly night and tell their grandchildren like the elders did in the days of yore. It is not a story to be told with the intent of reconstructing the past. And it is not a common, but the uncommon.

There are those relatives, and friends alike that may find it difficult to believe much of what I reveal in this book; but I am not in the least concerned because, whether I am believed or not everything I write herein is true. Much of what I reveal in this book may shock and anger many individuals, particularly my immediate family. I risk becoming an outcast to them by writing these things and this makes me hold back much of what I should reveal. I bear this risk in the belief that what I say may benefit other fretful teenage girls.

True, there are many women of all races who fell victim to such unusual circumstances of life. True, these women are unwilling to relate or reveal such innermost information about themselves.

But I will!

My problems seem to have started with one principal entity, a total lack of understanding between my husband and me. The saddest thing is that the misunderstanding was mostly on his side. He just didn't seem to understand, or care, what went on in my mind, especially the deep-felt love that I held for him. But, then, does any man understand what goes on in a woman's mind?

Often it is said, and it is a known and proven fact that a marriage between people will not long survive where one distrusts or manufactures false ideas about the other.

Let it be said that I was not "touched by an angel" in the early days of my life. I too had my shillyshally ways of doing things.

Chapter I

Caged Bird Set Free

I was born September 12th, 1962, the seventh of twelve siblings. We grew up in the coastal town of Gulfport, in the state of Mississippi.

Gulfport is located on the Gulf of Mexico, halfway between New Orleans, Louisiana and Mobile, Alabama. It is approximately 400 miles from Atlanta, Georgia, and has the distinction of being the gateway to the new South. It is a city with 26 miles of a white sandy beach. The subtropical climate has an average temperature of 68 degrees... 52 degrees in the coldest months. Gulfport has more than 50,000 tourists each year. Its recreational facilities encompass: fishing, sailing, golfing, tennis, sports, casino gaming, et al. It is particularly noted for succulent fresh seafood, and tropical flowers. Azaleas grow abundantly and probably more beautiful than elsewhere in the country.

My parents were deeply religious, firm, and unyielding in their demands for household respect and obedience. I had to follow their instructions to the letter. My repetitious routine was school... home... school ... home... school ... home. I was not even permitted use of the telephone to neither call nor receive calls.

I was thirteen years old when my father's disciplinary actions weakened to the extent that he granted me permission to attend a high school football game with my sister. I leaped with joy. My heart fluttered like a caged bird just set free.

* * * * * * * * * * * *

Over 23 years have elapsed since I went to my first football game. It seems that time passes as swiftly as the mind perceives it to happen. Little did I know that the would-be father of my future children and I would meet there. Jim and my sister's boyfriend, Perry were Pals. They were standing in a crowded area chattering away like two excited squirrels that had just rescued some falling popcorn from the ground.

I was situated amidst a group of noisy people. My eyes were wandering in a large circle and suddenly locked onto a man that was staring at me like a hungry wolf looking at a juicy beef steak.

His smile was gentle and reassuring. I lowered my

eyes self-consciously. My entire body appeared to have been seized with a mysterious paralysis and an aesthetic feeling of joy. I had never experienced such inner excitement before now. I stood glued to the ground and manage to muster enough energy to return his smile.

Jim motioned for me to come over. I was somewhat shy, but soon found myself ditty-popping toward the two of them. Perry introduced me to Jim, who asked, "What is your name? You look so much like your sister Jenny that y'all could pass for twins."

I replied in a trembling voice, "My name is Melody."

He held my hands. With a very delightful weakness, I fell under his spell. The earth began to melt beneath my feet. My pounding heart beat faster and faster; I thought it was going to exit its nesting place from within my chest. I felt as if I were holding the whole world in my hands. I was as happy as a thirsty kitten following a leaky milk cow. He continued talking, but his words just reverberated in my head. I couldn't understand a thing that he was saying. My mind dissolved into large droplets of love and lust. I was floundering in an ocean of pure pleasure.

Was this madness? Weakness? Foolishness? Irresistible love? What confusion led me to this ecstatic state of insane delight? Was this some idiosyncrasy of my heat oppressed mind? I was only thirteen years of age.

Jim was tall, handsome, with a muscular physique, and displayed a personification of herculean strength and vitality. He was dressed in casual clothing, typical of what one would expect to see at a football game. He sported an afro-style hair cut with a comb stuck right in the middle of it.

Where the average teenager of my age would see a stranger, I saw in Jim, a man of dignity; a man with an aspiring future. Many other ravening glances were cast in my direction, but I ignored them. Bewitchingly, I said to myself, *I have found the father of my future children, and I will do anything to get him.*

My Secret Rendezvous with Destiny

"Will you give me your telephone number?" Jim asked in a questionable manner. 'Do you have any friends?"

Reluctantly, I consented, and embarrassingly explained that my father does not allow me to receive phone calls or go dating with men. "I really don't have any friends,"

I said shyly. "My life is lonely." I gave him my phone number because I didn't want to lose him. However, I imposed the restriction that he was not to call me before 8:00 P.M., and only on Fridays. That was the time my father left home to attend his weekly ceremonial meetings. He did not return home until Saturday at 2:00 AM. Jim agreed to abide by my restrictions.

I waited with an impatience that was thinner than a single strand of silk for his first phone call. It finally came two weeks later. I could hardly conceal my wild excitement. My face lit up like the northern star in a clear ebony colored sky. I reacted as if I had just been given a 500cc injection of adrenaline and enthusiasm combined.

These secret telephone conversations continued off and on for nearly a year. My heart became saddened. I grew lonely. I was a living a lonely life. There had to be a way for me to see Jim face to face... to hold him... to kiss his gorgeous lips. I began to devise a foolproof scheme that would surely elude detection by my ever-loving father. I knew all too well that my life would henceforth be that of a horrid contrived nightmare if ever my devious plot were to be exposed. But, then, why worry. Be happy. My elder brothers and sisters were engaged in their secretive adventures. They would not dare expose me.

I grew a year or two older...but not necessarily wiser. I became bold, daring, and wilder than I should have been. The door of my destiny opened. An irresistible force shoved me right through it.

Jim and I initiated our clandestine social engagements. While my father was leaving by way of the front door, I was simultaneously climbing out of the rear window. We would meet a short distance from my home, about half a block away where Jim's mother would drop him off; he was under no restrictions as I was. We would return to my home for a bit of amorous embracing, caressing, and kissing.

I was completely lost in exhilarative pleasure and excitement when I held Jim in my arms for the first time. I was as happy as a buzzing honeybee in a field of sunflowers. I felt as if I was floating on a heavenly cumulus cloud when his strong arms reached over to embrace me. Suddenly, a strange feeling of uneasiness crept up and down my spine.

* * * * * * * * * * *

The inevitable was soon to become a reality. The invisible shackles that deprived me of my freedom were unleashed with a spectacular display of great pleasure and delight.

Jim's birthday, February 10, 1977, was only a fortnight away. I wanted to buy him a gift, but my piggy bank was as dry as a bone that might be found in the sands of a windswept desert. I kept asking myself over and over again, what could I do for him? I already knew the answer to my question.

Jim and I got brave, so to speak, and made plans for our first official date. In consonance with our preset time, he arrived at my house in his parents' old dilapidated station wagon. It closely resembled a vehicle that was used to convey the dead to the grave. I was not the least deterred, but I did feel somewhat squeamish about riding around in an old hearse-like automobile.

The night was cold, and a bitter chill surrounded our car like an ominous fog. We drove around and through just about every nook and cranny in the city of Gulfport.

"Let's go riding on the beach," he said, in a voice filled with intrigue.

I replied, "Okay with me. I know exactly when my parents will return home."

I had an insatiable desire for Jim. This would be a night of self-revelation, a night of remembrance. I gave no thought of what my future would be, and I didn't speculate over what was in store for me.

The temperature must have been near the freezing point, but my blood was like a boiling cauldron of tense emotion. He attempted to shield me from the cold elements of winter with his coat. I snuggled up to Jim so close that I thought I was on the other side of him. His arms encircled my body like the tentacles of an octopus. He began to kiss me. I eagerly returned his affections.

Jim asked in an assuring manner, "Do you want to climb in the back of the station wagon and lie down for a while?"

At first, I was hesitant. Then I thought to myself, why not?

We climbed in the back of the vehicle together. He gave me a slight push on my hinder most part to speed me over the seat. I felt very close and very special to Jim. We started kissing each other in a feverish manner that grew more intense and emotional with each passing second. I lost all track of time.

He held me tightly in his arms and began to kiss me on the neck. His fondling hands caressed my body with an awesome and incredible tenderness. An unearthly fear began to creep into my mind. I knew what this love play could lead to and I told him, in short breaths, to stop; but neither he nor I could contain our emotions. This was show time! He began to unbutton my pants. I longed for his touch and fondling to continue with every shivering muscle my body. I longed for him as a thirsty desert traveler longed for even a drop of water to cool his parching tongue.

Again, I was almost overcome with shock and uttered a grunting gasp of fear. Feebly, I tried to push him away. My will power melted into nothingness. My arms tightened around his neck, and my body strained savagely against his own. He thrust deeply inside of me. I let him drown himself in my virginal purity.

Except for a minor pain, I was as happy as ten thousand nightingales singing at the midnight hour.

A highway patrol officer pulled up alongside of us. The officer poked his head inside our vehicle with his blinding flashlight aimed right in our faces. We had just barely consummated our rendezvous with destiny. He wanted only to know if we were stranded and needed help. We had no difficulty convincing the officer that we were okay. He drove away without any further questions. Envisions of being labeled a "jailbird" danced in my head.

Crisis

A sudden icy fear gripped all the floating limbs of my body. I felt as if I had been propelled backwards through time, to the ice age of the dinosaurian creatures. My mind was in a frantic state, thinking about what my father was going to say and do to me for having snuck out of the house for the purpose of engaging in an illicit affair with a strange man. My very soul was painfully agitated in anticipation of the reaction of my family and friends, once my "spooky" adventure became public knowledge. Would Jim tell? Or boast of his accomplishment to his friends?

I resumed my routine of school, home; school, home; school, home. After all, there was nothing else for me to do.

Rumors began to fly around the school like butterflies in the spring; they spread throughout the neighborhood like hordes of locust in a field of corn. Humorously speaking, I overheard a group of students who were engaged in a bit of girlish talk. They were chattering away like parakeets in a cage. One of them said, "There's Melody now." They began to chide me in a mild and teasing manner.

Another said slyly, "Oh no! It couldn't be Melody;

her father wouldn't let her set one foot out of the house with a boyfriend. She still has her cherry."

Screaming hilariously with laughter, another girl said, "She might still have her cherry, but it has been pushed so far back it looks like a tail light."

Well, it didn't take long for the rumor to reach the ears of my parents that one of their daughters was pregnant. My father instituted immediate measures to squelch the rumormongers. He confronted my sisters and me with three empty baby food jars that had been labeled with each of our names, respectively, and asked us for a specimen.

I really didn't know much about the facts of life... didn't know anything about biology and chemistry ... didn't know anything about the birds and the bees except for the scarcity of information that I had discerned from my friends in school. Foolishly I asked him, "What is a specimen?"

He replied sternly and disgustingly, "Go piss in this bottle!"

Embarrassed, I lost my temper and irresponsibly replied, "You go shit in your hat!"

I had gone too far this time; there was no profound reason for my senseless thoughts.

Lo and behold! It was my bottle that came back positive. To my surprise and horror, I soon learned that I was two months pregnant. I was only 15 winters in this world; Jim was only 17.

I could feel my flesh, trying hard to crawl right off my bones. Panic seized control of me. My brain induced a strange internal feeling within me; I felt as if I was spinning around and around in a large whirlpool circle of fear and anxiety. I was lost in deep thought about what the future held for me. What was I to do?

My parents were looking angry and worried. A silence invaded the room like a thick blanket of fog; it melted away immediately when my father yelled in a thundering voice that seemed to shake the very foundation of the building, "My God, child! Why did you go and do this for? You are barely 15 years of age!"

I seized the opportunity to be the first to notify Jim that he could claim fatherhood within a seven-month time frame. He became very excited and expressed a premature fear of becoming a parent at such a young age. In a voice of mixed emotions, he said, "I'm going to let my parents know that you are pregnant." Neither Jim nor I were ready to become parents.

With an attitude of a sickening dislike, my father called Jim's parents and informed them that their son had violated his child's sanctity, holiness of life and character, and that she was in a terrible mess of trouble.

Jim's parents made a bold, determined, and courageous effort to assure my father that their son would be man enough to face up to his obligations and that his daughter and the baby would not be neglected in any manner.

My father was a doubting Thomas. He was as stubborn as the rock of Gibraltar. He enlightened them of the fact that he was fully aware that the foul deed committed by their son was not an involuntary act and that no legal actions against him, as pertaining to statutory rape, would be pursued. He further emphasized the fact that both individuals of concern, age 15 and 17, have no means of caring for an infant child. Therefore, arrangements would be made to secure adoptive parents as expeditiously as possible after the baby's birth.

I have always had the highest degree of respect for my father's wisdom and his unselfish love for all his siblings. However, when he talked about my unborn child being given up for adoption at birth, my mind exploded with an incredible anger and bitterness toward him. He made me feel a deep sadness, but I also had a feeling of pride of becoming a mother. My immediate reaction was equivalent to that of a raging bull. With an earth shattering, shrilly, scream, I said, "My baby will never be given up for adoption!" I will do anything and everything within my power to support my baby and myself!"

His negative attitude changed abruptly. I felt the spirit of triumph invade my soul... I would keep my baby. I thanked him profusely for letting me do so without a fight, but I may have added another wrinkle to his brow.

This day seems to have been the longest day of my life because of the surprised revelation of my gestation, hard fought decisions, and other very strenuous activities. I laid down to sleep with the hope of ridding my body of the yet undefined demons running rampart in my head; galloping like a race horse without a rider.

I awakened from my nightmarish dream before the cock had crowed three times to signal the beginning of dawn. I peered out of my window to get a glimpse of the morning star shining brightly in a dark sky. I listened to the birds singing in a choir-like fashion. Eight minutes later, the first rays of light from a slowly rising sun trickled through the tree leaves.

I decided to go for a morning walk. I walked slowly along a grassy pathway. Each blade of grass, heavily laden with dew, stared upwards toward my face, as if trying to read my troubled thoughts. A cool breeze caressed my brow. A feeling of uneasiness crawled over me like a thousand centipedes. I turned around and sauntered back toward the house.

* * * * * * * * * * *

I continued to live with my parents... nowhere else to go. There were many whispering conversations throughout the neighborhood about me. My parents became utterly embarrassed with the shame that I had brought upon them. And too, I think they were deeply hurt at having failed me as parents. They seemed as if they wanted to subject me to a Magnetic Resonance Imaging scan to determine the quantity of sawdust on my brain. I was disbarred from going to school and all church functions. I was beginning to feel very lonely and void of friends.

Chapter II

Dawn of A New Beginning

The young life within my body continued to develop and grow. I was given the best medical care that my parents could afford.

The days became nights and the nights became days in a rapid succession. They appeared to just merge together; it was like in the land of the midnight sun. My strolls from home became less frequent; when I walked along the side of the road I had more eyes on me than a truckload of Idaho potatoes. My outer garments conveyed the impression as that of a weather balloon being slowly inflated underneath them with hydrogen gas.

* * * * * * * * * * * *

There were many sleepless nights as I lay in bed, tossing and turning, trying to plan my future... trying to make plans for caring for my baby. Jim's relationship with me grew as sour as stomach acid and colder than the barren plains of the North Pole. The bonds that once bound us together had been severed. He developed and cultivated affairs with other young girls. There was nothing I could do to slow him down. I was as helpless as a young antelope being chased by a hungry female lion. I suppose he wanted to add another trophy to his collection.

Nevertheless, my love for Jim remained a beautiful endearment to my heart; my love for him was also pathetic. There were times that I wished he'd be run over by his own car.

The flame that once burned brightly to light our pathway of love had not yet been totally extinguished for he made numerous inquiries concerning the wellbeing of our unborn child.

La 'Shonda Elonda

I did not realize that the time for bearing my child was so close at hand. It was customary for my caring father to accompany me to the doctor's office for my routine physical examinations. During my visit on November 6th, 1978, the doctor displayed an alarming expression of deep concern. Again, and again he checked my blood pressure to be convinced of the results registered by his sphygmomanometer. I had a gut feeling that something was very seriously wrong with me, or my baby.

The doctor summoned my father into the examination room and said, "Your daughter appears to have developed a serious case of blood poisoning known as Toxemia. She must be hospitalized immediately for further tests and treatment." He added, "If we don't take corrective measures immediately, the bacterial toxins will enter the blood stream in a magnitude that would surely be detrimental to the baby."

My due date was not until November 21st, 1978. I could sense a dark cloud looming over my head. Fear ripped through my body like an armor piercing shell would tear through a tank on the battlefield. Intuition told me that the countdown to the hour of my childbirth was approaching rapidly.

Although I had not heard from Jim for a while, I refused to let myself sink into a puddle of quicksand of imaginary pride. I called him from my hospital bed, the same night, and informed him of the latest events pertaining to my health and condition. He was quick to respond to my telephone call. Perhaps the embers of his love for me had not completely died out.

Jim, along with his parents, came to visit with me a short time later. I was extremely happy to see them, and I felt myself falling deeper and deeper into a trance of joy and elation.

I waited with a false humility for him to break the thick silence that had filled the room to an overflowing capacity. It was so quiet that I do believe that one could hear a pin drop on a ball of cotton. I could almost hear his heart beating like the sound of a rumbling thunder. He was obviously uneasy and didn't know what to say to me. He just stared at me with downcast eyes and nervous glances.

I opened my mouth to speak, but closed it instead, with sobs of fear. Mentally, I commanded him to look directly into my eyes. Suddenly his voice shattered my heavily burdened thoughts. We talked. We talked about the things that we would do after the baby was born. His parents enthusiastically agreed to accept my baby and me into their home.

I said to Jim, "My eyes look upon you with love in my heart. We can now face the future without having to bear any shame that may be brought on by gossiping neighbors. Our family shall grow together. We shall face whatever awaits with courage, dignity, and perseverance."

* * * * * * * * * * *

Jim and his parents stayed with me at the hospital for quite a while before they left. Approximately thirty minutes after they left, I felt a sharp pain in my abdomen, and then another, and then another. I didn't know what was happening. An uneasy mood besieged me. My roommate, who had experienced the pains of childbirth, said, "You are in labor." She rang for the nurse without any hesitation or further explanation.

Fourteen hours later, I was the proud parent of a baby girl. She was born November 7, 1978 at 6:45 am. She weighed in at seven pounds and nine ounces. I named her La'Shonda Elonda Scott. She was an infant of incredible beauty, the loveliest baby that I'd ever seen.

My face lit up like the Eiffel Tower on the eve of Y2K, and my eyes glared with a spectacular brilliance of sparkling light when Jim and his parents entered my room at the hospital to take baby La'Shonda and me home with them. It was a day that will live in infamy.

The baby was dressed in a cute little pink outfit and she was shielded from the elements with a pink blanket. She was as beautiful as a "Barbie Doll." Her smile was indicative of someone who was well aware of what was going on.

I was homeward bound and chirping like a baby squirrel that had just learned to maneuver the branches of a tall oak tree. I mentally rejoiced at my successful adventure of having rescued Jim from the clutches of some unknown "she devil."

We received a warm and enthusiastic welcome in our home away from home, but I knew all too well that it was only a temporary residence and that I would be treading on soft ground in a strange and unfamiliar environment. Not unlike any other young mother, I dreamed of having a place that I could call my own little pad.

The time had come for me to activate my metabolism and regain my strength and energy, for there was much work to be done. My whole world had changed from a vast emptiness to one equivalent to that of an active volcano belching fiery lava of joy and excitement that scorched the tongues of all the rumormongers.

The whole family started making plans for celebrating Thanksgiving Day no sooner than we had settled down in our new home. I was not the least bit shy, even though Jim and I were not yet husband and wife. I toiled relentlessly like the minute and hour hand on a clock. I just kept going, and going, and going, with little thought given to the time of day or night. I experienced the meaning of perpetual motion.

Thanksgiving Day was celebrated in a traditional southern style fashion. The table was laced with the finest of linen, silverware and dishes. The extravagant menu included: turkey stuffed with seasonal dressing, country cured ham, collard greens flavored with cured ham hocks, diced yellow turnips, green beans, corn fritters, home-style biscuits, mashed potatoes, and yams. The desserts included sweet potato pie, apple pie, banana pudding, assorted cakes, and ice cream. A variety of soft, and not so soft drinks were plentiful. There was a bountiful supply of food for the family and close friends. It was truly a day to be thankful for, and a day to be remembered.

Then, we all started preparations for Christmas Day. My baby had gained weight in a proportional manner. She grew lovelier by the day. I disbanded the notion of placing her beneath the Christmas tree for fear of someone mistaking her for a gift, and just walking away with her. My only regret is not having pictures to attest to this most wonderful day.

We were truly blessed by Our Lord and Savior, Jesus Christ.

* * * * * * * * * * *

I was only 15 and knew little or nothing about the

facts of life, the ways and wiles of the world or the meaning of the word responsibility. With two fists full of determination, true grit, and a strong-willed power, I returned to school in quest of my high school diploma. It was not an easy chore because I held a full-time job to earn money to help support my baby and me. Also, Jim had a full-time job.

I lived at the home of Jim's parents for two long years amid good deeds, bad deeds, and ugly deeds. If I were an artist, I would paint a picture of my soul so that the reader could see all these deeds recorded therein. Otherwise, they shall remain invisible to the human intellect, even eternity. Let it suffice to say that there were times when my life seemed to be only a hollow balloon, until I filled it with hope, faith, and love. I became strong and as unfaltering as a lighthouse in a storm to guide my baby and me along a pathway of righteousness.

A lexicographer is a person who records and catalogs the behavior of words in their natural or native environment. I learned a few choice words, which, I believe, could be added to Merriam-Webster's Collegiate Dictionary. I think I could qualify as a lexicographer in this sense.

* * * * * * * * * * *

The days, weeks, and months staggered by like an "old drunkard" trying to find his way through a 30-foot garage door. After a lengthy battle, I finally graduated from Gulfport High School in June 1982. Victory was mine! I strutted around like an Indian Peacock and made a conceited display of my hard-earned diploma for everyone to see. It was prerogative to admire it openly.

Surprise! Surprise! Surprise! Jim surprised me with a new automobile for a graduation gift. Was he trying to soothe the pain and misery that had cloaked in silence for the past four years? Whatever the reason, I was elated beyond my wildest dreams. Tears of joy and happiness trickled down my cheeks like raindrops rolling off a sunflower leaf in the spring. No one had ever been so kind to me before.

We had been living in our own pad for approximately two years. I was 19, Jim was 21, and La'Shonda was four years old. The apartment costs $67.00 per month plus utilities. It was not a paradise, but it served the intended purpose.

I was a full-fledged adult now and would henceforth sink like a lead brick or swim like a friendly dolphin. The journey to my future had really begun. A voice within me whispered, "You are no longer living in a home away from home, this is your home."

An uneasy feeling caressed my brow. The thought as to where Jim got the money to buy me a car disturbed me. As the old saying goes, I was not about to look a gift horse in the mouth.

Marriage

We had lived together in the form of a common-law marriage for four years. The mere thought of it caused a gnawing pain in my stomach like a beaver chewing on a white birch tree. The tree would collapse and fall sooner or later, as would our relationship. I wanted for us to be united in a religious ceremony, with the hope that we would grow and prosper together. My persistence and perseverance were well rewarded.

We were married November 28th, 1982, in a small ceremony at my father's house. Only my family and few friends were in attendance.

It was illogical and unnatural for Jim to exclude his parents and other family members from the wedding, but I had long since learned not to question his motives and deeds. I suppose he had his own personal reasons for not inviting them.

When he finally decided to inform them of our

marriage, there was more hell raised than a woman scorned. It was a bitter pill for them to swallow. They reacted like someone taking a stroll through the devil's sanctuary without a roadmap to find their way out.

I trembled with fear at the thought of future repercussions that were as certain to happen as sure as thunder follows a streak of lightning. Instinct warned me that the primary target of their wrath would be me: I wish that my thoughts were wrong.

* * * * * * * * * * * *

Thirty days of physical abuse were heaped upon me as my wedding gift. Joyful bliss was gone; the beginning of my marriage consisted of disappointment, dislike, disillusion, disrespect, and deep regret. Visions of flashing daffodils floated in front of my eyes and I could feel myself falling into a deep, well illuminated abyss and floundering around in a red muck of depression. What evil had wrought its ghost upon my floor?

A plan was devised to escape my plight and inflict pain upon Jim at the same time. I put distance between us by running away to Union, South Carolina to cry on my grandmother's shoulders. After two weeks, I realized that running away was not the solution to a very serious problem and that I had become the victim of my revengeful plan of hurt. I returned home to mend the holes in our broken marriage.

It was compulsory for me to convince my doubtful parents that our marriage would work. Like a sledgehammer falling on the head of a railroad spike my parents drove home the point that neither Jim nor I were ready for marriage, and we lacked the responsibility and initiative required to raise an infant child.

Yes. We broke up but turned right around and made up.

* * * * * * * * * * * *

We were together again, but it should have been my legs that stayed together; I had two abortions in 1983. Jim and I agreed to the abortions because of our struggle to raise our first child. My fourth pregnancy culminated in the birth of a boy child, February 8, 1984. He was named Daymion Carvell Jackson.

Dark shadows of evil continued to lurk in my pathway of life and an unknown fate pursued me like a hound dog chasing a rabbit. We toiled and struggled, relentlessly against all odds to provide the proper care for our two children. Many unpleasantries were exchanged between us day after day and night after night.

Money was the predominant factor of our

discussions. On payday there was never enough money to meet our minimum expenses. The tone of our voices became unnecessarily volatile and words were harsh. Our imagination ran rampant and clutched at each other's throat in a threatening manner. We lived like a tempest in a teapot. The lid blew its top when Jim grabbed his coat and hat and said, "I'm outta here!"

This split up came soon after Daymion was born. Our marriage was on again, off again like a light bulb being turned on and off by a child in mischief. I was right at the borderline of being a poverty case. I just could not cut the mustard with my meager earnings. I applied for and received government assistance and moved into a low-income housing project. My rent was only $5.00 per month. Jim lived in his own separate apartment.

As the old saying goes, my head was bloody, but unbowed. I stubbornly refused to throw in the towel and continued the fight for my rights. Although separated, Jim and I maintained a sort of sporadic communication with each other. We would meet from time to time with the hopes of fitting together the scattered pieces of the jigsaw puzzle that constituted our lives. Our two children were foremost on my mind. I stepped my head took control of the reins.

Moving Up

Our last meeting was carried out under a flag of truce. It reminded me of Geronimo and the "Great White Father" puffing on the peace pipe. We kissed and made up. We were together once more.

I was utterly surprised, shocked out of my wits, flabbergasted, and even dumbfounded, when Jim told me that we were going house hunting. I flung on my whatchamacallit and away we went, making tire tracks around the community, in search of our dream house.

Within a relatively short period of time the paper work and mortgage loan were approved. We moved into our castle February 26th, 1986. He swept me off my feet and carried me through the portal to another world. Right then and there, he made a vow that his family would never be poor again. It was truly an overdose of delight. I imagined myself soaring high into the sky, like an eagle gliding on the currents of time, and casting an infrequent glance, a bird's eye view, at the chains of poverty that once held me tightly in its grip. Ideas were swirling around in my head like colored glass in a kaleidoscope.

We brought some nice furniture and other nice things to decorate the house. Jim even bought a new car. He really had big plans for his family. With the sauntering of time, we began to add additional rooms to the house to get more living space.

Then, strange things started to happen. For reasons unknown to me, Jim did not come home for long periods of time. Eventually, he told me that his new job required a great deal of travel and that he might be absent from home for even months. I would just have to learn to cope with it in order for him to fulfill his dreams of a better future for all of us.

It didn't take much effort for me to be coerced into quitting my job that paid less than minimum wage. Bare necessities of life taught me unusual kitchen skills. Before I could spell gastronomical temptations, Jim was out the door to institute the necessary action for the purchase of a building that would launch me on my way to becoming a restauranteur. It was ironic that he purchased the building where my parents formerly held their Friday and Saturday night meetings.

The source of Jim's intriguing wealth continued to alarm my curiosity, but I dared not to become inquisitive for fear of repercussions that were sure to follow. I had long learned to go with the flow.

The Brownstone Diner

The building was unoccupied at the time of its purchase. It was remodeled and renovated to accommodate 12 rooms upstairs and complete restaurant facilities downstairs. The Brownstone Diner became a reality.

The diner opened in 1987 with the customary fanfare as provided by a group of friends and relatives to wish us success and prosperity. The 12 rooms upstairs were rented for a modest fee that proved to be a good source of extra income.

My sister Jenny and my sister-in-law were employed as waitresses. They were each paid $100.00 per week. My brother, Kenny, was the custodian.

The hours were long, tedious, and demanding in every sense of the word, but I loved it, mainly because I was fortunate enough to be with my husband more often. The diner became a regular hangout for Jim and his friends. I soon became accustomed to burning the midnight oil and burning the candle at both ends. Nevertheless, the lengthy nightmarish hours did not prevent me from seeing after my two youngsters. I picked them up from school and brought them to the diner to be with me while I worked.

The Cruel and the Cruelty

Some of the finest food in town was served at the Brownstone Diner. The menu always displayed a variety of tasty food suggestions. Prosperity loudly rapped at the door, and widely we opened it. It was all too good to be true. An uneasy feeling clung to my body like static electricity clings to one's outer garments. I felt as if I were walking around in the eye of a fierce hurricane, where the winds are soothingly calm.

In spite of our successful business adventure, my husband began to exhibit an attitude toward me that was as sour as stomach acid. I had no idea what caused his mysterious actions.

The physical abuse that he heaped upon me way back in 1980 had returned in a manner more violent than ever. It reminded me of the movie "The Return of the Living Dead." Only a few people knew of the suffering that I had endured. I tried to maintain a shroud of secrecy in this regard, hoping upon hope that things would get better instead of worse. Neither my parents nor Jim's knew the reason for the unexplained facial contusions that were impossible for me to conceal. I just didn't want people to conjure up ill feelings toward my husband. There were times when Jim displayed a triple personality towards me: the good, the bad, and the ugly.

He would react violently if I didn't tell him the truth about some insignificant things... insignificant to me, perhaps not to him. He would interrogate me like a prosecuting attorney would do to a criminal on the witness stand. I became both irritated and extremely fearful of him; I would resort to "little white lies" in my own defense. These "little white lies" could very well have been the cause of my punishment, but I don't know.

My legs became wobbly, and I felt like the weight of the whole world had descended on my shoulders. I needed a confidant, one to whom my intimate secrets could be entrusted. My sister-in-law seemed to be just the right person, but time proved that I was dead wrong in my judgment of her. Everything that I told her came back to haunt me by way of my husband. She methodically reported everything that I told her to Jim, and probably added her own two-cents worth. Then, the pummeling was renewed.

I was soon convinced that the entire family had turned against me. Their respect for me was similar to that of a caustic acid being poured on an open wound. They became ambitious and ruthless. I listened, in total disbelief to outside rumors that Jim's family was plotting and scheming to take control of the diner and cast me out to the wolves.

Early one morning, I opened the doors to the diner, aided by beams of light from a lazy old sun. As the day waned on, I began to hum a jolly good note to the tune of "Oh Happy Day." It was nearing time for me to prepare basic foods for the lunch hour. My sister-in-law became very obnoxious and vehemently disagreed with my choice of foods to be served. She began to taunt and insult me.

Other members of her family were there but uttered not a single word until we became locked in what appeared to be mortal combat. I fought like a vicious wildcat and was winning the skirmish until all her family joined in the fray against me. I could not cope with all of them. I quit fighting, threw down my hand full of hair, and surrendered to the odds. I called Jim on the phone, and he arrived within ten minutes.

Jim assumed the role of judge and jury; he convened what is known as a "kangaroo court." He listened to explanations from both sides and ruled in favor of his family. I lost the battle and lost the diner in one concurrent action.

I knew I was finished. I snatched my food permit and license off the wall and yelled angrily, "Ya'll want this damn diner, ya'll can have it!"

I ran outside screaming with hurt, confused, and

saddened grief. I said to myself, I am going to leave this bastard, because he does not love me, he only loves his family! I couldn't remember a time I had not loved Jim, but right now I wanted to plant him on the other end of the grass.

* * * * * * * * * * *

Life is like an onion, peel off one layer at a time and sometimes it makes you weep. — Carl Sandburg

The diner business collapsed in total failure within four months after being taken over by my husband's family. Jim and I mutually agreed to lease the building for $500.00 per month. I went to work at Lowe's of Gulfport in the credit department.

Mercy! Mercy! Mercy, Lord, mercy! What sin have I committed to deserve the wrath that was continually being heaped upon me? I began to feel like a soulless rag doll toy that a young child had mutilated and abandoned. I felt hopelessly lost in a thick, thorny, wilderness with no way out.

I had been working at my new job for about four months. On the eve of Thanksgiving, I left work early; I was all excited about preparing a scrumptious dinner for my children. They were occupied with watching a television program in the den. Suddenly! Up pops the "devil" himself! Jim started interrogating me like a carpenter bee boring a hole in a slab of wood. I deliberately ignored his conversation and continued with the preparation of my dinner. I didn't want my holiday spoiled over some profound nonsense. I was stirring my pot of vegetables when Jim walked up behind me and without warning, struck me with a devastating blow to my ear with his powerful fist.

I reeled and staggered uncontrollably, like a boxer in a ring who had just been dealt a knockout punch by his opponent. I regained my balance, crying and moaning in a voice that expressed incredible agony. I looked at him amid blinding tears and asked sobbingly, "Why are you doing this to me?"

Slowly, I wobbled away from the stove and managed to seat myself on a kitchen Barstool, with tidal-wave tears rolling down my cheeks. Chills of fear embraced me from limb to limb. Roaring like a jungle lion and snorting like an enraged bull, he continued asking me questions about things of which I had no knowledge and therefore could not respond.

I clenched my jaws and held my breath, heedless of the next blow that smashed into my face and sent me reeling off the kitchen stool. The next thing I remembered was the dull crackling thud of my head hitting the floor. I lay there sobbing and gasping for breath like a fish stranded on a sandy beach. I was slowly being drowned by my own salty blood and mucus. The room started to spin around like a plane in a tailspin dive, and then there was darkness.

When I regained consciousness, my vision was jumbled and blurred. I had been placed in the bathtub and could feel sticky blood all over my clothing. Jim was bending over me with an expression of horror and astonishment. Still dazed, I could not figure out his expressions. Was he horrified because he thought that I was no longer among the living? Was he astonished that I could endure so much wanton punishment without ever fighting back defensively? How could I counter attack? I was a mere weakling compared to his strength. And too, I was a nonviolent person. He seemed to be fond of inflicting pain upon me and delighted in my suffering.

He scooped me up out of the bathtub and placed me roughly in the car. I thought, this is it; he was going to plant me among the roses. I didn't even have a chance to say goodbye to my children.

I was rushed to the emergency room of the hospital, where he must have stated that I had been drinking while driving and had suffered a terrible accident. The nurses treated me with a great deal of indignation and proceeded immediately to summon the police.

When the officers arrived, they began to question me about an automobile accident. I told the officers that my wounds were inflicted upon me by my husband, and not by a car accident, even though I looked and felt like I'd been hit by a diesel engine. I went on to explain that my husband had just given me the worst beating of my life.

The officers wanted to know if I would like to press charges against my husband on the grounds of assault and battery. I declined to do so for fear of repercussions against my family. A voice within me seemed to whisper, what fools we mortals be.

I could have easily qualified as a candidate for Hope House, a domestic violence shelter.

A New Twist of Fate

My life became a leaf-littered path of misery. There were many times when I imagined myself standing on the edge of the world and gave considerable thought to jumping into the bottomless pit, but I had to live for my children.

There were tears in my eyes and bitterness in my

heart. Call me an asshole, but I think my parents should have raised me better... perhaps I should have listened to them. For some strange reason, I was beginning to form an indifferent opinion about my father who once remarked that my marriage would never work. Had he placed a curse upon me? I think not. My father was a wise man then and he is now; I was beginning to suspect that he was absolutely right.

Fate dealt me yet another cruel blow. I discovered that Jim was having an affair with a young, beautiful, mulatto lady by the name of Portia. She was immediately regarded as my bitter rival. Why would he leave me? She could offer him nothing more than I had already given, which was my whole soul and body.

I felt as if a samurai sword had pierced my heart. My husband was my very life, and he was the only man for whom I had any love. I did not relish the prospect of losing him to another woman. I would use all my might to get him back for my children and me. Like a blind man in a new place, I had to feel things out. I could not go on as being merely a brainless housekeeper.

Misery indeed loves company. I was duped into obtaining a license and to open and operate the MCM Lounge in Bay Saint Louis. After the club was established and earning money, I was kicked out and replaced with my husband's family and I was barred from participating in any other activities concerning the club.

The lounge became a "hangout" for Jim and Portia. Like a wicked witch of the south, she lost no time in casting a magic spell of charm upon his defenseless mind. She actually lured him away from his home and family. I endured indescribable pain and humiliation as a result of his actions, even though he continued to provide needful things for his family... we were abandoned, but not forgotten.

If it's not one thing it's another. One night Jim came home and told me that he was being investigated by Federal Agents for some illegal activities. He further stated that the agents had given him an ultimatum to cease and desist his suspicious wrongdoings or leave the city immediately.

Jim did not elaborate further, and I didn't dare ask any questions for fear of being on the receiving end of an unwanted fist aimed toward my head. I had sworn to myself that if he ever strikes me again with anything harder than a piece of Kleenex he would be in hell before the devil knew he was dead. I meant every word of that statement.

We waived goodbye to Gulfport and said, "hello" to the spacious city that seldom, if ever sleeps, Las Vegas,

Nevada... also, my old "stomping grounds."

I never knew in the past and I don't know now, just what manner of man Jim was. He lavished the children and me with exotic trips to Hawaii, the Bahamas, Disney Land, and other places noted for fun, thrills, and excitement. We were having the time of our lives. He left us in Las Vegas and returned to Gulfport. I suppose he left us to continue his adulterous love affair with Portia.

We lived with a friend of mine that I had met some time ago. Eventually, I found work as a change girl in one of the casinos. As a matter of fact, I was doing exceptionally well in Las Vegas, with my work and gambling winnings. I soon located a house that was well suited for my family. I was about to take the necessary action to get my children enrolled in school, but just couldn't wait to call Jim and tell him the good news.

Hellcat! Hellcat! Hellcat! When I called Jim on the phone that "hellcat" Portia answered with a deceitful, "Hello." I had an uncontrollable urge to yank her right through the telephone line and wring her neck clean off her miserable body. She had taken possession of my husband, and now my home! I thought I was hallucinating ... having a nightmare! I slammed the phone down on the receiver so hard it sounded like the backfire of a diesel truck.

That "son-of-a-wandering-coyote" had served me with a plate full of propaganda BS and modern-day jargon about the FEDs chasing his ass out of town. He obviously went to some extreme to get rid of me to be with that feline cat woman. I hope she was blessed with nine lives because one of them belonged to me.

When my flaming temperament had fizzled out, I called Jim the next day for an explanation of what was going on at my house. He flat out refused to tell me anything. The fumes from my anger and resentment filled the whole room. Reluctantly, I asked, "Are you going to put the house up for sale and move to Las Vegas with us?" Why did I ask such a foolish question? His point blank answer was, "No!"

Grief stricken and sad I said, "Send me my car and me and the children will stay here."

He seemed to be annoyed with me. Growling a pregnant gorilla, he said, "I am not sending you anything!"

I was tired of his cheap shots and told him that we would be headed for Gulfport on the next plane flying that way.

What manner of woman am I? I had become only a figment or creature of Jim's imagination. I was only a "thing" in the service of the man I married. He treated me as a puppet, and jangled the strings at his pleasure, often to see me suffer from unimaginable agony.

My uncontrollable urge was to return to and deprive him of his virility. No! I would bury them both alive in some brightly illuminated hole, where they could see each other as they cherished their last infinitesimal breath. Our relationship had been spread so far apart that there was no chain long enough to bridge the gap between us.

Dark violence was driving me insane. Should I return to try to live with a person that inflicts random torture upon me so unmercifully? Was it jealousy? No. It was not. I just wanted revenge for being made the town's silliest clown.

On September 19th, 1990, Jim and Portia celebrated the birth of a baby girl. That was it; I was ready to quit. I just didn't how to cope with a husband who had conceived a child with another woman. For a period of time, I did not allow my children to go near Jim or the baby. However, my attitude changed, and my children were permitted to interact with their half-sister. After all, the child was not at fault.

Chapter III

Revelations

Fire! Fire! Fire! A voice rang out with such intensity that my eardrums reverberated like the strings of a bass guitar. The rapping at the door was so violent that the pictures on the walls became disoriented. I awakened my husband and leaped out of bed; my feet were in a running motion before they touched down on the floor. I raced frantically toward my children; my first instinct was to get them to safety. It was the morning of April 1st, 1991.

"Hellfire!", I said." This was no April fool's joke." When I opened what was left of the front door, an FBI agent thrust a search warrant in my face and asked bluntly, "Where is Mr. Jackson?"

I stuttered frighteningly, "Why? What?"

Local police and men wearing jackets labeled FBI and DEA swarmed around the house like bees on a honey tree. My mind was vaporized with all those officers and the news media; there were more flashing lights to be seen than those of a 3-ring circus. My rib cage flexed involuntarily from the pounding of my heart within.

They searched each one of us, including the children, and barked orders for us to go outside. We were placed under guard like criminals. Then, they proceeded to search the house and everything in it. My chest was aching badly, and I asked one of the FBI agents if it would be okay if I took the children to their grandmother's house, because I just didn't want them to witness what was happening here. Permission was granted.

I was not knowledgeable of my husband's private affairs and really didn't know what the raid was all about. It was not necessary for a hammer to fall on my head to learn that the agents were looking for evidence related to illegal drug activities in our home. Jim had shielded us from such activities.

To the best of my knowledge, no drugs or related drug paraphernalia were found, however, the agents discovered $80,000 and some very expensive jewelry in my husband's private safe. They confiscated the money, jewelry, and boxes of records that might possibly be used as evidence in a court of law to prove that he was a drug dealer.

Even our home was put under seize by the law; unbeknownst to me, a raid on our place of business was being executed at the same time.

This hellish nightmare prevailed from 6 a.m. to 12 noon. When the FEDs had gone, every floor the house resembled the streets on 5th Avenue in New York after a confetti parade. Jim's facial expression became distorted from pain, anger, and humiliation. I knew right then that a pack of wild horses could not keep him in Gulfport.

We collected our wits about us and lost no time in consulting with our attorney about instituting legal action to repossess our home. Surprise! Surprise! He too was under investigation by the authorities for some illegal activities. We ended up hiring an attorney from New Orleans, who was successful in pleading our case.

Our home was leased to a very caring family. Once again, we bid adieu to Gulfport and au revoir to Atlanta, Georgia. I felt good about moving and heading for the big city, I'd had a belly full of Gulfport.

We arrived in Atlanta in October of 1991 and went directly to an apartment that had been selected for renting. When we opened the door to inspect the premises, the roaches greeted us in a manner that seemed to resent our disturbing their privacy. We apologized by stomping the life out of the ones that came our way. The place was so littered with filth that by comparison a pigsty would have been a more desirable place to hang your hat.

After four hours of the grueling task of driving around the city in search of a decent place to live, we finally located suitable living quarters in the Turtle Creek Apartment Complex, but we had to pay six months' rent up front. Normally, one only paid one month's rent and security in advance. Being exhausted and disgusted, we readily complied with the landlord's request.

We settled down, got the children registered in school, and constantly chatted with our friendly neighbors. Everyone was happy except Jim. He was as restless as a fly caught in the web of a spider. He was pining for his family. The speed at which things happened actually dazed me. Jim's brother, sister, and other members of the family migrated to Atlanta without any hesitation. His attitude changed, and he rapidly adjusted to his new habitat.

The city of Atlanta really fascinated me. Jobs were plentiful. I rotated from one job after another in search of higher wages and better working conditions. There were moments when I simply lay down, relaxed, and listened to my inner thoughts. I peered into my future and saw a dim view of the unexpected. I sat up as if to get a closer look and gleaned a path that I should follow, but I knew not where. My thoughts were beginning to deceive me, and my vision became blurred. I was awakened from this hypnotic trance by the sound of a woodpecker perched high along the trunk of a tall pine tree that loomed ominously over my head.

Not the Common but the Uncommon

I continued to be happy and enjoyed some of the natural pleasures of life. Nevertheless, I seemed to have been entrapped in a routine rut of day-to-day living, as time passed by in slow motion. I began to seek out new adventures, more challenging tasks, and greater opportunities to fill a void that was growing within me. *A void? Within me?*

A mirrored reflection of my sanity set off an alarm my biological clock that alerted me to the fact that it was already past time for me to act. However, I was totally confused, and knew not what to do. I asked, "What must I do, when must I do that? What shouldn't I do?" I sought solace in prayer to alleviate my anxiety and needed no urging to do so.

* * * * * * * * * * * *

Each day of my life was more beautiful than the next; however, today seemed to be exceptional. The splendor of the rising sun quickly erased all traces of a hesitant dawn as the rays of light illuminated the morning dew on each blade of grass. I rewarded my lungs with deep breaths of fresh air, walking along briskly to loosen my straining muscles and to invigorate my thoughts of the previous day. Vain attempts were made to recreate the blurred vision of a path that I should follow to... I knew not where.

As the day waned on, I sat in my living room alone, in silent prayer. An eerie feeling of uneasiness sprouted within me like flowers in the spring. The nerves in my body, from my head to my toes, jangled discordantly. The room became strangely electrified and a hushed silence, like I never witnessed before, pervaded the atmosphere within.

Suddenly, the Spirit of the Lord was revealed unto me. He allowed me to view my entire life in a manner as clear as if I were watching a movie on a television screen. I looked and listened for a while and then held my head in my arms, trying to silence the voice and blot out the scenes in front of me. I closed my eyes for fear of what else I might see. I willed my eyes to open wide again, but they only grew numb and weak from trying to discern the figure in the room.

I was in grief and great sorrow because of the life I was living; my body was drenched in tears and cold sweat. Then, I experienced a transformation from anger, grief, and sorrow to an elated feeling of an indescribable peace between my body and my soul. It was then that the Spirit of the Lord said unto me, "The time has come for you to serve me and to devote your life to me. I will lead you along a path to follow, to one who is already in my service."

I told my children what had happened and said, "We are going to church this coming Sunday, but I do not know where yet." God works in mysterious ways, His wonders to perform. My sister-in-law called me and said, "I know just the church that you should attend." She made three such calls before I accepted an invitation to attend the church of her faith, which was the Tabernacle of Faith Christian Church. It is my strong belief that the three calls made by her were in the name of The Father, The Son, and The Holy Spirit.

No sooner than I had entered the hall of the Tabernacle of Faith Christian Church the Holy Spirit enveloped me and I felt good all over. I just couldn't be still. It was July of 1993 that I put my life in the hands of the Lord and asked Him to be my Lord and Savior. It was, by far, the best thing that I had ever done in my whole life. I remember these words from school: good, better, best; never let it rest, until your good is better and your better is best.sr

Reverend John A. Davis, Sr. was the pastor of the church. He taught me faithfully for six years. My children and I became Born Again Christians. We loved to do the work of the Lord. My husband had not yet become a servant of the Lord; he had not been born again. The Word of God says in 1 Corinthians 7:14: For the unbelieving husband is sanctified by the wife, and the unbelieving wife is sanctified by the husband. Matthew 6:33 says: But seek ye first the Kingdom of God, and His righteousness; and all these things shall be added unto you.

After giving up my house in Gulfport I became lonely and weary of living in the apartment. I prayed three times a day, asking God for His mercy and His blessings in helping us to acquire our own home in which to live. My prayers were answered. We were able to get an FHA loan approved and moved our new home December 23rd, 1993. We celebrated Christmas Day by giving thanks to the Lord. When fortune knocks, open the door.

Prison

The dawn of the New Year collapsed and fell on its face, scattering shards of bleakness throughout and around the house. Jim received a federal indictment to appear in court, in Biloxi, Mississippi on January 27th, 1994, to respond to charges that had been filed against him. In a sense of unexpected horror, I read a portion of the indictment and staggered slightly; it dealt a severe blow to my heart. Tears rolled around in my eyes like steel ball bearings.

I knew what the indictment meant to the family; it was frightening to say the least. A futile attempt was made to clear my dizzy and my spinning head. Jim was literally dumbfounded. I tried to cheer him up with a little womanly companionship. In the meantime, Jim's brother had received a similar indictment. They went to court and entered a plea of not guilty.

We returned home and resumed our normal status of living, as if this fiendish nightmare was not real. My mind became less efficient with each passing day. My husband and I became stretched out to the maximum. It was not enough that the government had confiscated all of our assets, but they were determined to send my husband to prison as well. How could we explain all of this to our children? We just prayed that the nightmarish monster would just vanish into thin air, like a puff of smoke.

I became more depressed, angry, confused, and bitter at the world. Jim seemed to be slowly drifting away into no man's land. A new wrinkle on his forehead was tale-tale evidence of his aging body and mind. The thought of going to prison had a toll on him yet he remained sufficiently strong enough to prepare us for the worse, which was sure to come, as sure as the sun rises in the east and sets in the west. I admired him for his caring thoughts.

Jim's trial date was approaching with all deliberate speed. His brother had already accepted a plea bargain with the state prosecutor, but Jim maintained his innocence and steadfastly refused to entertain the thought, even though all other associated with the case had already done so. This alluded to the fact that the prosecutor would entice the co-defendants to testify against him.

Jim engaged the services of an attorney that painted one bright picture after another, but to no avail. When the money well went dry, so did the attorney. Jim then asked for a court appointed counselor and received one. After considerable discussions had taken place, the counselor convinced Jim to enter a plea of guilty. The prosecutor offered Jim a condition of 20 years in prison without a trial, which was flatly refused.

We traveled to Biloxi, July 19th, 1994, for Jim to undergo a test for drug use. When we arrived, Jim was told to have a seat, and someone would be with him shortly. After about 45 minutes, my heart started beating with such fury that I thought it was going pop right out of my blouse. Intuition warned me that something was definitely wrong. I could sense and feel it. I stared at Jim with fear protruding from my eye sockets; my hands were wet with perspiration. Jim asked, "What's wrong with you?"

"Nothing is wrong with me," I replied nervously.

Jim asked again, curiously, "Then, why are you looking at me like that?"

Precisely at that moment, I tore my eyes from Jim and saw two big burly agents and walking briskly in our direction. Their focus on us was unwavering. They approached guardedly and asked in a grime tone, "Are you Jim?"

"Yes". Jim replied in a trembling voice.

Forthwith, one of the agents slapped a pair of handcuffs on his wrist and said, "We have a warrant for your arrest."

I screamed vehemently and shouted out, "What are you doing? He just came here for a drug test." I continued to scream at the top of my voice, as they led him to the elevator. I screamed and screamed until the cords my neck was about to snap. I tripped over my own feet and fell to the floor in a crumbled heap. I began to grasp for breath. A uniformed officer came over to me and politely asked, "Ma'am, are you alright?" He touched my shoulders in a gesture of assistance. I panicked and looked at him in anger and hatred, as if he was the one who had just taken my husband away from me. I yelled out, "Take your hands off me; all you folks want is to put all black men in prison." The officer said defensively, "Ma'am, I was only trying to help; I am sorry if I have offended you."

I fumbled in my purse for my car keys, picked up Jim's personal items that the two agents had given to me, glanced at the officer with contempt and ran to my car still screaming and muttering, you heartless...

I stopped at the nearest pay phone and called Jim's mother to tell her what had happened. She asked calmly, "Where are you on your way to?"

"To the attorney's office," I replied.

She said, "I'll meet you there."

"Okay" I mumbled and hung up the telephone. There was so much water in my eyes that I seemed to be looking at the world from of a goldfish bowl.

* * * * * * * * * * * *

The visit to the lawyer's office was fruitless. He called the Probation Officer to determine the reason for Jim's arrest and was told that the judge revoked Jim's bond because he had been tampering with government witnesses. The lawyer readily admitted that he had only advised his client to gather information that could be used in his own defense.

My temper flared as hot as the devil's handshake. Any legal beaver should know that it is wrong to go near a government witness, let alone talk with one. We stormed out of his office like a locomotive out of control down a steep ravine. We were finished. Our defense lawyer had committed a terrible sin in the eyes of the law.

The next day I went to the jailhouse to visit Jim and to tell him why his bail bond had been revoked. We talked via a telephone intercom and faced each other through a thick plate glass window. I touched the glass with the palm of my sweaty hand and he did likewise. I told him that his trial would be held soon.

We only had thirty minutes to talk, but I squeezed in a one-hour news update. The prison guard barked sharply, "Time's up." The phones went dead. I waved goodbye to Jim. When I walked out, the door slammed shut making a sound like that of a Civil War cannon being fired. I knew then, why a jail was nicked named the "slammer."

Once outside, I looked back at the many inmates with their hands sticking through the steel-barred windows and wondered if Jim was one of them, waving goodbye to me.

A few days later, the court granted Jim a bond hearing to determine if his bail bond should be restored. Just about every member of his family was present. I testified on Jim's behalf, but it didn't help. The prosecutor used every means at his disposal to keep Jim incarcerated. He was successful. After almost one hour of testimony, the judge ruled that Jim was to remain in the custody of the state, due to the manner in which he violated his original bond ... witness tampering. Jim was handcuffed and led away by the court officers amid screams from his family. I was no exception. I could have easily qualified for the nickname of "cry baby."

My anger and crying were inseparable, like two peas in a pod. I finally out did myself by committing a very foul, stupid, senseless, and vile deed. I vented my anger on God, saying, "Why God? Why God? You told me that Jim would be set free." I must have gone insanely mad!

I stayed in Gulfport until August and returned to Atlanta to get my children registered for school. Immediately, they began to ask for their daddy. I could not gather enough courage to tell them what had happened. They would find out soon enough. I just told them that he was in jail and that he would not be returning home for a long time. Common sense dictated that I should have explained right then and there as to why he was in jail, but I didn't. As time went by they became so vigorously inquisitive and concerned that I had to explain everything, in meticulous detail.

* * * * * * * * * * * *

Jim's trial was scheduled for January 10th, 1995, after having served six months in jail... this was "D-Day." His family, my pastor, church friends, my children, and myself of course, were there to offer support.

Jim entered the courtroom in an unusually calm manner, in anticipation of his freedom in every sense of the word. He was elegantly dressed in a new suit, shirt, and tie, in contrast to the usual orange-colored prison garb. His shoes were highly polished ... spit shined. He wore a clean-shaven expression with a neatly trimmed haircut. An exuberant smile of confidence cloaked his face. The children waived and called out to their daddy in sympathetic tones. I sat there in a tremulous state of mind with a great deal of apprehension.

The court attendant shouted, "All rise." The trial judge came into the courtroom and sat down; he banged his gavel so hard that I thought the handle had broken; court was in session.

The prosecutor stood prominently in the middle of the floor. His eyes seemed as hard as a synthetic diamond and very uncompromising. I was utterly surprised, but unshaken when he called me as his first witness. He took aim at me with his mouth and fired question after question at point blank range. There were moments when his voice boomeranged like thunder, but I was not deterred. He paused occasionally, as if to remember his manners, but I don't think he ever possessed any. His sole and determined purpose was to send Jim "up the river" for 20 years. Jim was permitted to testify in his own behalf.

After listening to Jim's testimony, the judge showed some leniency and did not put him away for the 20 years as sought by the state prosecutor. Before sentencing him, the judge proceeded to tongue-lash Jim in a long-winded speech that I thought would never end. The final verdict; he was sentenced to 10 years in federal prison.

A guard slapped a pair of handcuffs on Jim and led him away. There was wailing, screaming, and gnashing of teeth by all his family. My neck must have swollen three times its original size because a lump suddenly developed in my throat that made it extremely difficult for me to breathe. Sobbing, I asked Jim's lawyer if he could arrange for me to see him, explaining that they wouldn't even let me say goodbye before taking him away. Permission was granted for me to visit him in his holding cell. We embraced, kissed, and prayed together.

The prison guard opened the door and told me that I would have to leave now. I tore myself apart from Jim, staggered out of the cell door, collected my children, rejoined my friends, and headed directly for my father's house.

My dad had prepared a scrumptious, southern-style dinner for all of us. Everyone was eating, making with loud laughter, telling jokes, rejoicing, and celebrating in a manner that they were glad the ordeal was over. Me, I couldn't eat a single bite of food because it swelled up in my mouth like a self-rising biscuit in a red-hot oven. After dinner, the children and I went back to Atlanta.

Ministry

We arrived home late at night, tired, weary, and worn. I bedded the children down and staggered through the doorway of my room. I pulled off my clothing. Slipped into my nightgown and flung myself backwards into a lonely bed and gazed up at the ceiling in despair and with a dark heart. The heart needs light, and without light it will not long survive.

I lay there in deep meditation, pondering, and contemplating our future, wondering where I could get the courage to go on. I couldn't bear the thought of having to raise my children alone for the next ten years. It would be better for me to be subjected to another 18 years of abusive beatings. I wanted to commit suicide. I would curse God and surely die, but I had to carry on my life for the sake of my children. I drifted away into a sort of twilight sleep.

It was mentioned earlier that the Spirit of the Lord had appeared before me and asked me to serve Him. Once again, the Spirit of the Lord set my soul on fire with searing flame that would not burn. He asked, "When are you going to serve me, now that I have taken your husband away from you? Will you preach My Word?"

I said to the Lord, "No."

The Lord replied, "Then, I shall cause a demon to invade the body of one of your children, and this child shall rise up against you."

Still, I ignored the Lord's words and warning.

A short time later, I noticed that La'Shonda was acting in a very strange and demonic manner. She gradually grew worse and completely lost control of her senses. She became extremely violent toward me. She hit me in the face with a torturous blow from her fist that sent me reeling backwards, with my nose dripping shamelessly with blood.

She was like a demon from the fiery depths of hell. She reminded me of the movie, "The Exorcist." The wrath of the Lord was surely upon me.

He spoke to me again and asked, "Now, will you preach My Word?"

The Spirit of the Lord departed with these words, "Now that you have accepted your calling, everything you touch will be as pure as gold."

After unwavering and incessant tutoring by my able-bodied pastor, Pastor Davis I was ready to preach my first sermon, 15 days after my husband had been sentenced to serve 10 years in federal prison.

I sat calmly in the pulpit alongside my pastor, with

my hands folded delicately in my lap. I looked out over the congregation and gleaned many eyes that were filled with anticipation and a few that appeared to be as hard as desert stones.

My pastor announced that I would be delivering my first sermon. When he completed his introduction with all his kind and flattering remarks, I arose and made a convincing approach to the podium, wondering if all those people were there to prejudge me. It didn't matter, because I could feel the Spirit of the Lord with me. A hushed voice came over the audience. My voice rang out, "The topic of my message is, Who Are You Going to Serve?"

After the completion of my electrifying delivery of the Word of the Lord, I received praises beyond my wildest dreams. I sat down and wiping the perspiration from my brow, said repeatedly in a low tone, "Thank You Jesus! Thank You Jesus."

I had been transformed into a new person, with a new meaning of life. This was January 25th, 1995. I have been in the service of the Lord since that date and will be forever more.

Chapter IV

A Prisoner's Wife

Often times my life displayed an impression of being recorded on video tape, presenting me with a mental opportunity to fast forward, reverse or pause. Manipulating the VCR control to any one of these three positions was more devastating than the other. It was sheer folly to view my future, too horrible to look at my past, and too emotionally disturbing to pause in the present. Nonetheless, life must go on; like a Broadway play, the show must go on even when the actor/actress is incapable of further performance.

Jim was transferred to a Florida State Prison in Marianna, Florida, after serving seven months in the local jail. After learning of his new location, I depressed the fast-forward button on my VCR control to hasten the date when we could visit with him, which was two months later (May 1995). Marianna is approximately four and a half hours driving time from my home in Atlanta, Georgia.

We arose early in the morning on the day of our previously planned trip to Marianna. The driving route had been carefully planned for us by my brother, Rudy. Gleefully and excitedly, we packed our car with food, water, clothing, and other items of necessity to sustain us on our long journey. The lazy old sun rose slowly in the eastern sky, brightly colored orange fireball, flinging rays of light every direction. As soon as the first beam of light creased my brow, I turned on the ignition to my car, released the brake, pressed gently on the accelerator and headed for Florida.

Before my children fell victim to the monotonous, sleep inducing hum of the automobile engine, I sang the old famous highway song:

At 50 miles per hour, sing the song: highways are happy ways,

At 75 miles per hour, sing: Nearer My God to Thee,

At 95 miles per hour, sing: Lord, I Am Coming Home.

They were soon fast asleep. I was alone, except for God. I prayed and asked His blessings for a safe trip to and from our destination, without harm or incident.

We arrived in Marianna and checked in at the only

motel there called the Hill Top Inn. It didn't take long to learn that all of the occupants of the motel were there for the purpose of visiting someone dear to them at the prison. Marianna was a small country town, void of any form of entertainment. This didn't bother the children any, because they were so anxious to see their daddy. Me too.

Visiting hours at the prison were from 8:00 a.m. to 3:00 p.m., we arrived at 8:30. I gazed upward at the ominous prison walls; it was the most ghastly, grim and ghostly sight that my eyes had ever beheld. My heart pounded laboriously within my chest as we approached the gate that resembled the one at the fabled Frankenstein's evil castle. Anxiety possessed my brain, my thoughts ran amuck, and my body was drenched with a cold sweat, just knowing that my husband was one of the many concealed from civilization by concrete, steel, and barbed wire.

After being divested of all our personal items, we were permitted entrance to the visiting room in a group. Then, we underwent 30 minutes of administrative procedures. Jim leisurely walked in. At first sight of Jim the children shouted out, "Daddy! Daddy!" They ran and leaped into his arms at full speed; the force of the impact caused him to stagger slightly. I let go of my emotions with indescribable screams of joy, not really knowing what I was saying. His strong arms encircled the three of us at the same time, and, then, individually. I could not restrain my emotions or my exhilaration of seeing him again, neither could the children. Jim's identity was Number 03673043, otherwise, no name.

Moments later, I put a bear hug on him that nearly caused his rib cage to buckle the Golden Gate bridge during the last devastating earthquake in San Francisco, California. The lid on my emotions was blasted off like that of a manhole cover.

The rules in the visiting facility were very strict. Jim and I were not permitted to touch each other after our first encounter. Photographs were permitted however. I must have had a dozen pictures taken just so I could hold his hand. We talked, and talked, and talked; he was mostly concerned about our welfare.

The children amused themselves with various games and play with the many other children there. Also, they enjoyed the use of the vending machines. It is of interest to note that visitors were not allowed to bring in any money larger than a five-dollar bill.

Sharply at three 3:00 p.m., the prison guard roared, "Visiting hours are over!" I grit my teeth in an unsuccessful effort to keep from crying. Tears rolled down Jim's cheeks like droplets of rainwater would slide off the hood of a highly polished automobile. Both of us tried in vain to conceal our sorrow from the children. I experienced a sense of difficulty in trying to distinguish between sorrow and anger. I was angry at the world for Jim being in prison and deeply sorry that I had to leave him there. "Parting is such sweet sorrow."

Upon leaving the prison gates, the steel bars seemed to stare at our hasty retreat. My body trembled in sadness and my imagination went uncontrollable; I could feel and hear the sound of those "wailing" walls.

We threw our belongings in the car in a haphazard fashion and departed the motel in a blaze of gloom. My watery eyes blurred my vision as we traveled the lonesome highway back to Atlanta. It would be a long ride home, perhaps the longest drive that I have ever taken.

The sun was rapidly setting in the western horizon and the intensity of the approaching darkness increased minute by minute. It was compulsory for me to get control of myself to avoid becoming a highway statistic. My son Daymion kept me awake with continuous conversation and questions while La' Shonda slept soundly, all the way home. He asked solemnly, "Mama, when is daddy coming home?" My only reply to his question was, "Son, I don't know yet."

When we arrived home, the moon appeared to be reddish in color because I was looking up at it through bloodshot eyes. We grabbed our bags and stumbled through the front door. The children went immediately to their room and were fast asleep before their heads hit the pillow.

I was exhausted after the long drive and the strain was highly visible on my face. My throat was parched like a half-roasted peanut. I extinguished the lights in hope that the darkness would provide me with a little relief from my overpowering anguish. I crawled into my bed like a centipede, tucked my head under my blanket, and just stared blindly into the darkness. I was still shedding tears and my eyes felt as if they were going to bulge right out of their sockets. I used my thumb to jam them back in their nesting place. My contorted face relaxed somewhat, but my pulse rate had increased from 72 to 92, as if I had been trying to run a four-minute mile. I drifted off into a deep slumber.

Ebbing Tides

We made monthly visits to Marianna over a period of four years, to see and talk with Jim. The trips were as methodical as a child in a swing ... going back and forth, back and forth. The opportunity of meeting new friends in the same situation, and gossiping about one thing or another, made it easier for me to deal with the pain of his incarceration.

We were financially stable because Jim had the forethought to save wisely, to be prepared in the event of some catastrophic situation as ours. I worked sort of part time at Clayton Community Services. My big break came, July 8, 1996, when the American Red Cross hired me. The pay and health were excellent and afforded me the opportunity to amply support my crew of two. The job entailed extensive travel, but that only helped me to get further adjusted to my living woes.

The holidays became my worst nightmare. I relegated myself to an off-line seat and torturously watched other families celebrate and make merry with their children and friends. I participated as best I could for-the sake of my children, but my husband was dearly missed, not being present to share in the festivities with us. Loneliness and sadness besieged me on each occasion. I can fully sympathize with any woman who has lost her husband, for whatever reason.

I have learned over the years to count my blessings. The word of God states: Philippians 4:11: Not that I speak in respect of want: for I have learned, in whatsoever state I am, therewith to be content.

I praise God in all situations. The only way to survive this chaotic world, is to let God take control of your life.

As fate would have it, my daughter became pregnant at the age of 19. Yes. I was disappointed because I wanted so much for her to go to college to better prepare herself to meet the challenges of this unpredictable society. At least she had the courage to come and tell me all about it. I immediately advised her to tell her father and be prepared for whatever adverse consequences that may follow.

To our surprise, her father expressed no anger, and assured and predicted, with a high degree of assurance that she would become a very good parent since she already had finished high school. La'Shonda felt real good about those encouraging words from her father.

Jim's Transfer to Atlanta

Jim and I had made numerous requests for him to be transferred to a prison that was closer to his family, to Camp Setting in Atlanta. His counselor, who vowed that such action would never materialize, emphatically denied each request. Nevertheless, I prayed incessantly that the counselor would change his attitude and initiate the necessary action to accomplish the transfer. My prayers were answered. I received a telephone call from Jim's cellmate who informed me that Jim was en route to Camp Setting, Atlanta. This was a joyful surprise that filled my heart to the brim with happiness. It was a great consolation to have him so close to home.

We were granted visiting privileges two weeks after his arrival at the camp. When we checked in at the visiting center, there were no metal detectors, no painstaking forms to fill out, and no of steel-barred doors to rattle the eardrums. Above all, we did not have to contend with that long drive to Marianna, FL. In addition to all the above, we were permitted to touch each other and hold hands as we pleased.

My son and I were at the prison camp promptly on each weekend except when my traveling commitments with the Red Cross dictated otherwise. My daughter's visits were less frequent since she was establishing and pursuing her own lifestyle and destiny.

* * * * * * * * * * *

Our ebbing relationship worsened with the outward

flow of time. It had its beginning when Jim was imprisoned in Marianna and grew worse when he was transferred to Atlanta; it became as sour and acrid as sulfuric acid. His bellicose attitude always left me with an empty feeling in my stomach. He would induce arguments over the most trivial things during each of my visits. His telephone conversations became so outlandishly cruel that oftentimes I would not lift the receiver to speak with him when he would call.

Jim was trying to control my life from his prison cell. It just couldn't work and just wouldn't be tolerated. I pondered; do all inmates try to manipulate their external interests and their loved ones in a similar manner? Was Jim an exception? It soon became extraordinarily difficult for me to carry on a conversation with him. Had he lost complete trust in me? What?

Many times, I had to bite my tongue, and control my temper to keep from saying things that I might later regret. My visits began to dwindle; our relationship reached its lowest ebb, strained to the breaking point, and we entertained each other with discussions pertaining to divorce. There was no other alternative.

Year '99

The events of the year, 1999, will be related in a non-flamboyant manner and not necessarily a chronological order. They may be categorized as being, good, bad, or ugly, as conclusively discerned by the reader.

An oversight on my part, but I became a grandmother in the year 1998. My granddaughter Genesis celebrated her first birthday October 20, 1999. The name Genesis means "beginning." Genesis, of course, is the introductory book to the entire Bible, and gives an account of the relationship between God and the human race. The love that I hold for my granddaughter is so great that it is beyond my capability to describe it.

The month of June marked Jim's first anniversary the Atlanta prison camp. We continued to have our ups and downs.

My son Daymion was sent to live with my brother, Rudy, and his wife, Maurica, who lived in Leominster, Massachusetts. I just couldn't provide the motherly attention that he so urgently desired and needed. Rudy proved to be an ideal model for my son, although it would not be an easy task for the two of them, since they were both working to fulfill their own family obligations. Rudy is very intelligent, with a great deal of common sense that most people lack. Among other talents, he is quite skilled in the use of computer technology and was sure to have a tremendous influence upon my son. They would, most assuredly, receive the blessings of the Lord for their good deed and sacrifices.

Rudy has served more than 15 years with the United States Air force. He was blessed with his request for an assignment at Warner Robins Air Force Base, Georgia only two months after accepting the responsibility of caring for my son.

A nagging pain developed my lower abdomen; I had tolerated and ignored it for almost six months. The intensity of the pain increased, and Jim scared me into seeing my doctor; I didn't need much coaxing, as the pain grew steadily worse. On September 9th, my doctor informed me that there was a fibroid, a benign tumor, attached to the wall of my uterus and that it would have to be removed by surgery. Well, a knife is a knife, is a knife. I decided to put my trust in God and my fate in the hands of the surgeon.

I applied for a leave of absence from my job with the Red Cross on October 28th. All of my bills could wait, but I was deeply concerned about personal assistance after coming home from the hospital.

My operation was performed successfully on

November 1st. The tumor was so large that it included an abdominal hysterectomy. My sister, Toni, stayed with me night and day while I was in the hospital. She too, will be most certainly blessed by God for her kindness and concern for my health. I will always be grateful to her, as well as her husband, who helped me tremendously in keeping my spirits high. I truly believe that all the good deeds unto me, was surely an act of God.

My sister was employed as a supervisor at the Biloxi Veteran's Administration and took time off from work to care for me. She stayed with me for seven days after my discharge from the hospital on November 4th. This time allowed us to talk about numerous things about the past, the present, and the future. It was a sad day for me when she left for her home in Gulfport.

Rudy and his family came to be with me during and after my operation. Maurica, my sister-in-law, was like an angel from heaven. She demonstrated an exceptional degree of compassion, love, and dedication of duty in catering to my every need, as if I were her own helpless child. She did so much that a feeling of guilt crept over me like a thick early morning fog, for she had to look after her own family as well. Maurica prepared all my meals, washed my clothing, and maintained the house in an immaculate state. She was very tolerant in listening to me complain the blues about my relationship with my husband, and all other woes that haunted me like an evil plague. She was a diligent counselor as well as my adorable and much needed nurse. Being firm in attitude is truly an understatement, for she commanded every ounce of my respect.

My daughter moved back with me, after independently pursuing her own way of life for approximately six months. She was not free to play the role of a nursemaid, she worked very hard to earn money to help me with my household expenses and to provide the necessary nourishments for her daughter, Genesis.

My Red Cross co-workers, friends, and other family members were exceedingly generous with their visits, kind words of encouragement and well wishes. Their showers of kindness poured out like Morton's salt. I would not have made it through this ordeal without God, family, and friends. My husband was greatly relieved to know that I was in the hands of many good people who were there for me during the total time of my recuperation.

* * * * * * * * * * *

Six months before my medical diagnosis, hospitalization, and surgery, a very unusual request was made of me by a voice from heaven.

In the wee hours of a morning following a day during which my labors left me totally exhausted. My body was resilient as an overcooked spaghetti noodle when I was awakened from a deep slumber, a sort of twilight sleep. The voice from heaven said unto me, "Melody, I want you to write a book and title it, 'Living the Life of A Prisoner's Wife.'"

I didn't put a pen between my finger and thumb to write a word on the book for more than half a year. The writing of my story, concerning my journey through life, had its beginning when I was sufficiently recovered from my operation. I often wonder if it was the way of the Lord to get me to honor His request. I will never again put off for tomorrow, the things that I should do today. I will never again disobey the word of the Lord.

* * * * * * * * * * *

My emotions began to wreak havoc upon my mind. I became depressed, disillusioned, and overcome with sorrow because my husband could not be with me when I needed him most dearly. And too, my physical condition prevented me from going to the prison camp. I was mentally locked in a prison within myself, with imaginary walls and steel bars staring at me and daring me to attempt to escape. Evil had wrought its ghost upon my mind, and the dying embers caused me to exhale smoke of despair.

Experience has taught me that the ways and means to survive the ordeals of *"living the life of a prisoner's wife"* includes: faith in God, prayer, love, understanding, patience, loyalty, dedication, perseverance, and hope. A prisoner's wife will not long survive, in the absence of these basic attributes of character. Friends and neighbors, alike, would often confront me with expressions of, "I know how you feel honey." No living person ever knew my true feelings. They cannot even imagine the difficult and trying times that I endured in my efforts to raise a young lad whose father was incarcerated in a nearby prison camp.

My son was approximately 10 years of age when his father was imprisoned. He is now in his late teens, and has become disgruntled, disenchanted, and depressed. My untiring efforts to assume the role of a father have been terribly disappointing and highly ineffective. Albeit, I have made a valiant attempt to teach him the necessity of being respectful: self-respect, respect for his family, respect for his fellow companions and respect for females of all ages.

Daymion gradually became withdrawn from me and

refused to discuss any of his personal problems; he just assumed that I would not understand. Perhaps he was right since I never understood his father, and probably never will. Whatever the cause, he became rebellious at times, like a wild stallion, and grew weary of listening to, "Son, don't do this and don't do that." His facial expressions told the vivid truth of how he missed his father, especially at baseball games, basketball games, and other father-son related activities.

I just wasn't good enough to assume the role of a father, and I doubt that I am alone in such matters. Sadness enveloped me to the extent that I wanted to go into hiding, just like an Alaskan bear in the winter, until my frustration had been washed away with the melting of the snow.

Proudly speaking, Daymion withstood many trials and tribulations to become a top-notch sportsman. He displayed par excellence in baseball and basketball. I am extraordinarily proud of both my children for having survived the terrible ordeals imposed upon them by misfortunes of life.

Each time that I went to the prison camp it was tantamount to entering the gates of hell, a place of pity, a place of despair, et al. I became obsessed with the observation of the sorrowful expressions of other visitors. Clearly etched upon their faces with an invisible ink, were the words, "Why Lord, why my family? Will this terrible nightmare never end?"

Next, my eyes just roamed automatically, like an infra-red beam of light searching a darkened sky for trivial signs of life, from one inmate to another, in slow motion, in search of something I knew not what. Their eyes bulged with glee and excitement when the visiting doors opened; in contrast thereto when the visiting doors were about to close, their eyes slammed shut in an effort to stem the flow of tears.

A prison, is a prison, is a prison. I per chance, overheard a conversation at the close of the hours; an inmate tearfully said to his wife, "I am sorry to see you leave and wish you could stay here with me."

The young wife replied quickly, "Hellfire, man! I love you, but I don't love you enough to want to live in prison with you!"

The prison camp overflowed with talented inmates. Their choir was exceptional and would offer worthy competition for the Morgan State University Choir. When their voices rang out in unison the Amazing Grace hymn the enchanting musical notes held the audience spellbound and sent small tremors through my soul like aftershock waves that follow an earthquake.

Divorce Action

The visitors to the prison included women and children of varying ages; there were both single and married women. I often wondered just how many of the married women contemplated and followed through with divorce actions. I did.

The frequency telephone calls increased in leaps and bounds and soon exceeded my capability to cope with them. Each one of them became angrier and angrier and so frustrating that my ears burned, my body screamed and squirmed, and my nerves were shattered into fragments of disgust and hatred. He called me at least ten times daily, as consistent as clockwork. If I was not home to answer his calls in sequence, he heaped punishment upon me with a tongue lashing so vitriolic that my knees would sag, and my head would throb.

My temperament grew more furious than the growth of jungle vegetation in the Amazon forest. Was he deliberately goading me into action to seek a divorce? Was his unoccupied mind running amok about some infidelity on my part? Perhaps his fellow inmates would fantasize with him about other men into my "sugar bowl." Perhaps he thought that I would do unto him as he had previously done unto me.

My husband said, repeatedly, "You don't how it feels to be in prison, locked behind bars from civilization."

I replied sarcastically, "I've been married ten years, and I'm still serving time."

I was almost overcome with a guilt complex, as a prisoner's wife that my husband was merely trying to earn money to provide sustenance for his family by the only means that he knew how. Should I have intervened to get him to cease and desist in his activities? The fact is, I did not know anything about his criminal activities. Whenever I became slightly inquisitive, he would use my head for a punching bag.

Despair, anger, and bitterness prompted me to file papers for a divorce. I felt as if I were running a race where the finish line kept moving farther away, where there was no ending. An imaginary sweat ran down my back, and tears flowed over my cheeks like water over the Niagara Falls. The sidelines were clogged with family and friends, cheering, and encouraging me to run a little faster; a little faster to where, eternity? They didn't seem to realize how tired I was and had no idea about how I felt toward running the race at all, and probably could care less. I didn't want to be the runner who reaches her goal and find that there is no other place to go.

Nearing the point of exhaustion, I wanted to give up the race, give up my marriage, just walk away, and free my inner soul from prison.

* * * * * * * * * * * *

The reality of being divorced set in a delayed shock from a terrible accident. We both felt the sting of devastation. I didn't have a husband and likewise, he didn't have a wife. It was an emotional time for us. What would I do now?

I informed the children of our state of affairs. Neither one of them displayed any reaction whatsoever. They merely assumed a "so what" attitude.

Ironically, my divorce papers had not been received after a considerable number of days had gone by. I decided to call the court clerk to determine the cause of the delay. After a bit of research, the court clerk called and stated, apologetically that she erred in the processing of my papers and that my request for a divorce has been a mere judgement of dismissal. This was December 1st, 1999. I called Jim on December 2nd and gave him the news that we were not divorced and the reason therefore.

Jim said, with a dry sense of humor, "Now you can resume your threats of divorce."

Epilogue

It is difficult, if not impossible for me to tell a story in a normal manner, the way a story should be told. I have withheld too many dastardly deeds during my journey through life. The difficult part has been accomplished; the impossible will take a little more time.

I have spent the last few years trying to regain my sense of humanity. I have learned to face life's hardships with a smile. I do not surround myself with a cloak of artificial pride. No amount of abuse can deprive me of the things that I crave for my children, and my children's children.

Making a few wrong turns here and there posed no problems, but when I took the wrong exit off my highway of life, the road sign read, "ONE WAY ONLY." I was doomed to a nightmarish hell.

I no longer shed tears for myself, I shed tears for other women throughout the world, wherever they may be, who have suffered or may be suffering similar indignities at the hands of cruel men who never thought once of the harm they inflict upon the souls of their victims.

Nothing can be said, and nothing can be done that will ever "take me away from my guy."

Jim will be released from prison the year 2001. Hope rises my heart.

* * * * * * * * * * * *

God gave to the world three fundamental gifts: Hope, Faith and Love.

The Gift of Hope

What is Hope? Hope is another cord that binds us to God.

Hope is a feeling that life has a meaning. Life without hope is an empty, boring, and useless life. Hope is a gift of God and fills our lives with the assurance of His purpose in good times and in bad. We should be thankful to God for the gift of hope. It is as big a gift as life itself. We should always carry hope in our hearts.

Hope is far more durable than the clothes we wear or the foods we eat and drink. The hurdles of today are but the training grounds of hope for tomorrow. Hope is confidence in God and our glorious future with Him, because we know that He loves us.

It is traditional with the young ladies to view a hope chest as a thing for storing sheets, pillowcases, linens, and things. There is a spiritual hope chest, a daily diary to record a word of prayer. We should often review and reread our words and be reminded of God's constant care for us.

Bring your hope chest to God. He will pull out the rags of fear, sorrow, and depression, and fill it with Himself.

The Gift of Faith

What is Faith? First and foremost, faith is belief and trust in and loyalty to God.

We all should be thankful for the gift of faith because faith is a living reality to one's life. Faith is a fidelity to one's promise.

We must stand firm in our faith and live by faith in the Son of God. A person is put right with faith in Jesus Christ. The righteous will live by faith. To be without faith is to be without life. We must be mutually encouraged by each other's faith.

The blessings you seek through prayer will be given

unto you by the Lord your and you will be successful in all your righteous endeavors.

The great kings of Africa ruled their lands by faith. The slaves of Egypt and the slaves of America were freed from bondage through their faith in God. Apartheid was abolished in South Africa by the faith of the masses and the faith of the many freedom fighters. Wonderful things have been achieved all over this earth by the greatness of faith.

Faith is the substance of things hoped for, the evidence of things not seen.

Faith is everlasting; your faith in the Lord should endure forever.

The Gift of Love

What is Love? Love is a manifestation of God: in similitude that a smile is the manifestation of joy.

Traverse the dark valleys of the voices of evil with the love of the Lord Jesus in your heart and your path will shine as bright as a morning star.

Heed the love of Jesus and serve Him with all your heart, all your soul, and all your might.

Endeavor to include your love for Jesus in all your daily deeds and His blessings will be bountiful.

God gave to the world three fundamental gifts: Hope, Faith, and Love: the greatest of these gifts is Love.

Instill the love of the Lord Jesus in the planting of your fields of fortune and reap your harvest in abundance.

Fear the Lord Jesus: for as high as the heavens are above the earth, so great will be His love for those who fear Him. True love is unselfish, loyal and benevolent concern for the good of your family, your community and your church.

Obey the commands of the Lord and He will surely keep His covenant of love with you. For comfort and peace of mind, proclaim your love for the Lord Jesus: sing of His love and His justice; walk in his ways; and He will surely crown you with His love and compassion.

Love your neighbor you would love yourself, is the second, greatest command of our God. Love is not love that alters, when alterations find or bends with a remover to remove.

Offer your love and friendship in response to those who would be your enemies, for love will triumph over evil.

Volunteer to convey the love of Jesus to little children, so that His love may continue through many generations.

Enjoy and cherish the three gifts of God; give pleasure to their abundance in a common bond of love and friendship.

About the Author

Melody M. Jackson lives in Atlanta, Georgia. She is the mother of two and the grandmother of seven. She holds a master's Degree in Adult Education. She continues to share the love of God with all she meets.

www.ingramcontent.com/pod-product-compliance
Lightning Source LLC
Chambersburg PA
CBHW072059290426
44110CB00014B/1752